FOUR SEASONS AT THE SHORE

PHOTOGRAPHS *of the* JERSEY SHORE

FOUR SEASONS AT THE SHORE

PHOTOGRAPHS *of the* JERSEY SHORE

Featuring the Work of Forty-Nine Photographers

Essays by Rich Youmans | Sandy Gingras | Larry Savadove | Margaret Thomas Buchholz

Prologue by John T. Cunningham

DOWN THE SHORE PUBLISHING

Harvey Cedars, New Jersey

The words "Down The Shore" and the Down The Shore Publishing logos are registered U.S. Trademarks.

Down The Shore Publishing Corp., Box 3100, Harvey Cedars, NJ 08008
www.down-the-shore.com

Manufactured in China.
10 9 8 7 6 5 4 3 2 1
First printing, 2004.

Book design by Leslee Ganss
Picture editing: Ray Fisk
Essay editor: Perdita Buchan

Library of Congress Cataloging-in-Publication Data

Four seasons at the shore : photographs of the Jersey shore : featuring the
work of forty-seven photographers / essays by Rich Youmans ... [et al.] ;
foreword by John T. Cunningham.
p. cm.
Includes bibliographical references and index.
ISBN 0-945582-91-9
1. Atlantic Coast (N.J.)--Pictorial works. 2. Seasons--New
Jersey--Atlantic Coast--Pictorial works. 3. Seashore--New Jersey--Pictorial
works. 4. Coasts--New Jersey--Pictorial works. 5. Beaches--New
Jersey--Pictorial works. 6. New Jersey--Pictorial works. 7. Seashore in
art. 8. Seasons in art 9. Photography, Artistic. I. Youmans, Richard,
1960-
F142.J4F68 2004
974.9'0022'2--dc22
                                        2004049341

Barnegat Light beach.

PHOTOGRAPH BY RAY FISK

To me, through every season dearest;

In every scene, by day, by night,

Thou, present to my mind appearest

A quenchless star, forever bright;

My solitary sole delight:

Where'er I am, by shore, at sea,

I think of thee.

— *George Macbeth Moir*

Contents

Beach heather, Island Beach State Park dunes.

Prologue

PHOTOGRAPH BY DAVID LORENZ WINSTON

Beach reflections, Stone Harbor.

This book of words and images properly fixates on the sights, the sounds and the power of imagination at the New Jersey Shore. Such sensuality is basic: anyone seeking enduring links to this stretch of seacoast finds them only when the senses come into full play.

I did not grow up by the Jersey Shore; I didn't even see it until a wild night in September 1934 when my brother and I drove down from Morristown to see the burning *Morro Castle* cast up to the very edge of the Asbury Park convention center. The roaring wind, the stinging of the hard-driven rain and the smell of a burning ship remain fresh in memory.

During my college years, my girlfriend's family invited me down to Manasquan on weekends for a full, if unspoken, examination. With her little sister, I dutifully combed the beach for seashells, pitted my macho teenage body against the breakers, and heard the sounds inside and beyond the flimsy walls of the bungalow (it was called that) where we stayed. I passed all examinations. In time, we married.

But full focus did not come for me until early in August 1955, when my editor, Lloyd Felmley, told me that my newest series on New Jersey for the *Newark Sunday News* would be on the New Jersey Shore. Like my three previous series — on the state's counties, its industry and its agriculture — this series, too, would become a major book published by Rutgers University Press.

"This is no joy ride," Felmley warned. "You must get to know the shore better than any outsider ever has known it. I want you to see it in all seasons, in all kinds of weather, in good times and bad. I want the history, I want the atmosphere, I want the big towns and the little burgs and I don't want anything that reads like a puff piece."

I could spend as much time as I needed, stay wherever I wanted, and choose my style of presentation. All I had to do after three or four months of research was write about twenty weekly articles of my own choosing, each about 3,000 words in length.

The day after Felmley's pep talk, my wife, our son, 7, and our daughter, 3, left for two weeks at Beach Haven. The last winds of departing Hurricane Diane buffeted the newly-completed Garden State Parkway as we drove south. The sky was the unstained blue that always follows a strong coastal storm. The atmosphere was as pure as if filtered through an air cleaner. The hot sun cast strong, enhanced shadows.

Hurricane tides had cut a three-foot-deep cliff along the strand and gouged deep channels through the beach. The first afternoon was a toddler's holiday, but another high tide smoothed away the cliff and tidied up the beach.

Each morning we explored the edge of the sea, seeking shells. To our three-year-old, every shell, scrap of shell, or even an old whelk case were treasures. She did not have to know the names of shells; her treasure was in the finding, not the categorizing — not a bad rule whether gathering shells or watching tiny sandpipers dart away from dashing waves, as if they dared not wet their feet.

On lazy afternoons I sat, flirting with sunburn and watching each wave roll in, rising, rushing shoreward, collapsing on the sand, then retreating to gather strength for the next assault. The implicit power awed me; the soft fizzing out soothed me. That summer, for the first time, I realized the peace that can be found in the regularity of the tides.

But autumn arrived. I strolled the beaches and the boardwalks in towns strung like jewels from Sandy Hook to Cape May. By day I haunted libraries and museums, seeking origins, seeking dates, seeking the historical why that enticed different generations to the Jersey Shore. History would be the vital flesh on the skeleton I was shaping from the sensuality that pervades anyone who seeks to understand the shore.

I walked dark, empty boardwalks in January, hearing only my echoing footsteps. In February I saw ghostly, flapping signs that recalled last summer's joys. I strode along beaches in spring and autumn, and witnessed the death of Atlantic City's tradition that snow never falls on the boardwalk: a December storm piled snow a foot high on the famed walk.

I spent a week in early November, gathering my thoughts in an almost-new, almost-empty, motel at then-desolate Wildwood Crest and swam, alone, every afternoon in the still-warm ocean. I readily agreed to a supposed shore "secret": that autumn is the greatest of seasons.

I became almost as one with the past — with Indians who came in summertime to harvest fish for winter months and to garner shells to make their wampum; with those who found God in the unrelenting waves and the gentle winds and founded religious camp meetings at Ocean Grove and half a dozen other spots from Atlantic Highlands to Cape May Point; and with those who came in the 19th century for the sheer worldly pleasures at Long Branch and the discreet, gentlemanly gambling in Cape May inns.

Notebook after notebook gathered my facts and my thoughts — and my sharpened senses retained the beauty and the wonder. When it came time to write, my first words were: Most important is the sea in all its ever-changing moods.

I wrote of the history, the boardwalks, the man-made pleasures, and the distinct regions of the shore, but I also dwelled on rewards that come from even a bit of adventuring — in sailing on Barnegat Bay, in seeking "Cape May diamonds," in exploring then-secluded Sandy Hook, in watching an osprey take flight, in walking for miles along the hard sand left by high tides, in watching snowy egrets seek food in the meadows, and in watching the sun go down across Delaware Bay.

Most important is the sea, free (except for beach fees) for anyone, whether he is down for the day or down for a few weeks in a multi-million dollar seafront mansion. Free, too, are the seashells, the saucy seagulls, the relaxed chatter from nearby beach blankets. The only requirement is that the senses must be given full play. The strand belongs more to the child who picks up shells than to the man who lolls away precious hours watching television on the most expensive and expansive beachfront deck on the coast.

The waves roll on, fascinating newcomers as much as they have enticed me nearly all my life. Wild storms strike, rearranging the shoreline in ways that no one anticipates or desires. Birds follow prehistoric spring and autumn migration patterns through Cape May and the wildlife refuges to the north, little fingers reach in wonder for a dazzling clam shell burnished by countless waves.

The Jersey Shore is, as always, what we seek, what we find or think we find, and if we stay with it, is always far more than we might have imagined.

— *John T. Cunningham*
Florham Park, New Jersey

Introduction

Barnegat Light.

This is a coast sun-drenched in memories, and our memories cement the shore in place and time. We hold them dear and protect them, to savor again, as if re-reading sentimental old love letters, for they often connect us to our youth and to a sense of freedom and of happiness. For each new generation, the appeal is fresh, and will continue to be so as long as the Atlantic waves roll along this coast's islands, peninsulas and sandy beaches. As we grow older the bond only strengthens, even as the shore changes.

This book is a document of a uniquely American place recorded in a transitional time. It is a gallery, of sorts. Or perhaps an album for a very large collective family whose touchstone has always been the Jersey Shore. Most of the photographs included in this book (gathered from nearly 8,000 images) were made over two decades since the early 1980s. Some were published in the *Down The Shore* calendars during those years, but many evocative images could not be accommodated in a calendar format and are seen here for the first time. Each photograph is a personal interpretation of a place, a time, a season at the shore. We've tried to include both the familiar and the seldom seen, the natural and the developed coast, for it is often this dichotomy that captivates us.

We don't presume to suggest that the more than 300 images in this book capture every aspect of the shore, or fully represent the personal shore of all who feel attached to this coast. But we've tried to include a full spectrum: in broad, wide-angle views and in narrow, specific details. We hope this conveys the essence of the New Jersey Shore — and, most importantly, the feelings and emotions it evokes for so many millions of people.

In his Prologue, John T. Cunningham observes that this is a sensual shore. It is a sensuality that changes with our activities, as well as with each seasonal shift of nature. The essays, by writers who have observed and chronicled the changes and the attraction of this coast, capture those moods.

The contributors to this book feel the shore's enduring allure, and offer their own interpretations of what the seasons at the shore — and our connection to it — mean. As much as words and photographs on paper can possibly convey the sights, smells, sounds, textures, delights, and feelings of a place, we hope you'll find the soul of the Jersey Shore here.

— Ray Fisk
Publisher

Herring gull, Beach Haven.

FOUR
SEASONS
at the
SHORE

Long Beach Island

Spring

PHOTOGRAPHS BY THOMAS A. MCGUIRE (above) and SALLY VENNEL (below)

Wildwood beach and pier (above).

By Rich Youmans

Deserted Beach, Sandy Hook

Once again, I return to this still-empty beach. Shorebirds wheel and glide, trailing their shadows along the incoming waves, their bellies inches from whitecaps. Glyphs of heron and gull track the sand, and wet shells shine in the noon sun. Behind and above me, rising from the Highlands like a medieval fortress, the fraternal Twin Lights — one square tower, one octagonal, both of a time long gone. Far across the Atlantic, the New York skyline serves as a hazy reminder of the world beyond. I walk on, caught between eras, between environments, between the ocean and the bay.

Not far away, holly grows hard against barracks that withstood two world wars, and the bird shadows flit over crumbling battery emplacements. Everywhere, divisions: human vs. natural, concrete vs. sand, eternal vs. ephemeral. Season vs. off-season. A winter chill laces the salt air, but so does the spring sun. The wind blows in off the great Atlantic, sending showers of spray, little hosannas. I feel it in my ears, along my raw cheeks. It penetrates my chest, and in so doing it hollows and cleanses me. In that moment, I am like a mirror through which this landscape processes endlessly: the white-crested breakers, the gleaming shells, the marram waving among dunes as if in celebration.

That is the special power of the Shore in spring, when a walk along the beach can be a personal journey — one that for many of us has become a sustaining ritual. Soon, no doubt, I will welcome the advancing crowds, the rush of energy that summer brings. But not now. I walk on, absorbed by this place and its elemental beauty.

The Boardwalk, Seaside Heights

Saturday morning. Along the boardwalk, winter shutters have been raised from the storefronts. Bicyclists thrum along the wooden slats, their jackets a dandelion yellow, a sky blue. A kite bobs and weaves overhead, tethered by an invisible string to a group of young boys, their wild hair blowing in the ocean breeze. Along the Atlantic, sunlight winks as if with secrets, with promises.

Over and back the long
waves crawl and track
the sand with foam.

— Hilda Doolittle

Surf City (facing); Holgate sand patterns, Long Beach Island.

The season is approaching.

The slow pulse of winter has quickened, and expectations grow. On one bench, an elderly couple sit side by side, watching the play of the kite against the clouds; he puts his arm around her shoulder, she puts her hand on his thigh. Young families walk in unison, teenagers huddle under lampposts, pigeons land and peck at pieces of pretzel, hot dog buns, taffy. Seagulls arc and swoop, while children jump from arcade to arcade, grow shrill against the background din of machine-gun fire, detonating missiles, the squealing of tires around hairpin turns. In the rear of one arcade, the solid thwack of wood on wood issues from the Skeeball lanes, and a middle-aged man smiles. Outside, a cyclist rings his bell for no reason, amid young laughter and old longings and the great hush of the waves as they roll in, roll on.

Spring Returns, Long Beach Island

Like the slow progression of the waves, weeks build to weekends, and each weekend builds upon the next. Every Saturday, the causeway becomes more crowded: a growing procession of sunburst metal, polished chrome, windshields bright with sun and sky. Along the boulevard, traffic lights no longer blink vacantly; instead, they resume their steady rhythms — red, yellow, green — as the traffic ebbs and flows, always building. Tarpaulined powerboats disappear from driveways; in gardens, fresh roses and hyacinth appear.

Gradually, the part-time residents reclaim their patches of sand, prepare for the summer to be. Windows are opened and screens replaced, rugs are hung and beaten clean. The ritual of restocking begins: fresh linens, silverware, a new color TV; pillows, paperbacks, charcoal briquettes. Volleyball nets sprout on lawns. Lines at the supermarket swell.

Each weekend, eyes watch the still-vacant driveways, wait for yet another return, the chance for reacquaintance. Each weekend, a few more houselights push back the darkness and streets take on a new glow.

Dawn Flight, Cape May Point

Morning's first light flares along the horizon. High above the breakers tumbling into themselves, the birds of the Great Atlantic

PHOTOGRAPHS BY RICK VIZZI (above) and SALLY VENNEL (below)

Footprints, Ocean City (above).
Adult and immature herring
gulls, Surf City (left).

23

Little Beach and Little Egg Inlet (right). Fort Hancock and Sandy Hook Light (below and facing).

PHOTOGRAPHS BY RAY FISK (above) and THOMAS A. MCGUIRE (below)

Flyway — falcons, ospreys, fish hawks — fill the brightening sky. Their wings silhouetted against the far blue, they soar by the hundreds, en route from South America to Greenland. Over marsh ponds, mud flats, estuaries, and bays, the raptors follow their migratory route.

Below them, in the shallows of Delaware Bay, another migration is taking place: Along Higbee Beach, horseshoe crabs return to lay their eggs. Their prehistoric carapaces gleaming along the strand, they deposit thousands of grain-sized eggs — pale green, tan, off-white. Like the raptors, they follow a timeless ritual, born of instinct. With the season's turn, their paths become clear.

And as the temperatures climb and spring edges closer to summer, another ritual continues along the nearby highways and backroads and causeways — all the paths leading toward the Jersey Shore.

PHOTOGRAPH BY MICHAEL S. MILLER

PHOTOGRAPH BY EDWARD M. KULBACK

Point Pleasant Beach snack shop (above). Steel Pier, Atlantic City, and Asbury Park Casino (facing).

PHOTOGRAPHS BY NANCY L. ERICKSON (above) and WILLIAM BRETZGER (below)

Morning: Atlantic City Boardwalk (above), Ocean Grove (facing, above), and Ventnor (facing).

PHOTOGRAPHS BY DAVID LORENZ WINSTON (above) and CHARLES ARLIA (below)

PHOTOGRAPHS BY REBECCA BARGER (above) and KEITH DREXLER (below)

PHOTOGRAPHS BY DONALD T. KELLY (above) and WILLIAM BRETZGER (below)

Atlantic City skyline at dusk (above). Lucy, the Elephant, Margate (left). Early morning, Ocean City: Boardwalk and surfer (facing).

And I have loved thee, Ocean! and my joy Of youthful sports was on thy breast to be Borne, like thy bubbles, onward.

— *Lord Byron*

31

PHOTOGRAPHS BY RICK VIZZI (above) and RAY FISK (below)

PHOTOGRAPHS BY RAY FISK

Installing channel markers, Barnegat Bay (left).
Cape May ferry, Delaware Bay (above). Bay Head
bed and breakfast room (facing). Ocean City
Boardwalk (facing, above).

PHOTOGRAPH BY RAY FISK

Ship Bottom, Brant Beach, Little Egg Harbor Bay from Cedar Run marshes (above). Tidal creek and salt marsh, southern Ocean County (facing). Boat and dock, Leeds Point (facing, right).

…This creek-indented and sea-beat region from Cape May to Sandy Hook — 100 miles — a stretch offering both the people and the places most interesting to my taste, in which salt and sedge are inborn.

— *Walt Whitman*

PHOTOGRAPHS BY DONALD T. KELLY (above) and WILLIAM BRETZGER (below)

Beach scenes: Cape May (above),
Ocean Grove (below),
Long Beach Island (facing).

PHOTOGRAPHS BY MELISSA MOLYNEUX (above) and PATTI KELLY (below)

Storm clouds move offshore, Cape May (above).
Bay Head (facing). Ocean City surfer (facing, below).

PHOTOGRAPHS BY JUDIE LYNN (above) and REBECCA BARGER (below)

The wild wind raves, the tide runs high, as up and down the beach we flit, one little sandpiper and I.

— *Celia Laighton Thaxter*

39

PHOTOGRAPH BY BOB MANNING

And here the sea fogs
lap and cling.

— *Rudyard Kipling*

PHOTOGRAPHS BY RICH A. KING (above) and JUDIE LYNN (below)

*Coastal fog: Island Beach State Park (above),
Point Pleasant Beach marina (left), and Sea
Girt Lighthouse (facing).*

PHOTOGRAPHS BY BURTON E. LIPMAN (above) and ROBERT MISEWICH (right)

I should have been a
pair of ragged claws
Scuttling across the
floor of silent seas.

— *T.S.Eliot*

*Horseshoe crabs mating: East Point,
Delaware Bay (right), Island Beach State
Park (facing), laughing gulls feasting on
the eggs, Cape May (above).*

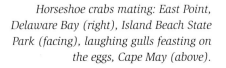

43

Shore birds on the Delaware Bay (above). Surf clams at high tide line (facing). Nesting piping plover (facing, right). Birdwatchers, Cape May (facing, bottom)

Gather a shell from the strewn beach and listen at its lips: they sigh the same desire and mystery, the echo of the whole sea's speech.

— *Dante Gabriel Rossetti*

PHOTOGRAPHS BY SUSAN HILL (above) and STEVE GREER (below)

PHOTOGRAPH BY MICHAEL J. KILPATRICK (above)

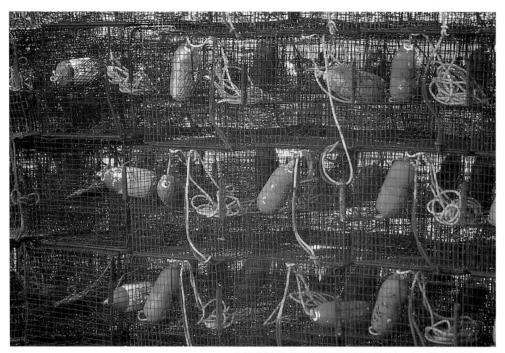

Commercial fishing boats leave Barnegat Inlet (facing). Sea King, *a 1963 scallop boat wreck, Barnegat Light (below). Crab pots, Motts Creek (right).*

PHOTOGRAPHS BY ROBERT MISEWICH (above) and RAY FISK (below)

Oak and triple bronze encircled the man who first committed a frail boat to the cruel sea.

— *Horace*

Mullet, Barnegat Light (above). Gillnet fishermen with bluefish catch, offshore Barnegat Light (facing).

They that go down to the sea in ships,
That do business in great waters;
These see the works of the Lord,
And his wonders in the deep.

— *from Psalm 107*

The fisherman goes out at dawn
When every one's abed,
And from the bottom of the sea
Draws up his daily bread.

— *Abbie Farwell Brown*

PHOTOGRAPH BY CORNELIUS HOGENBIRK

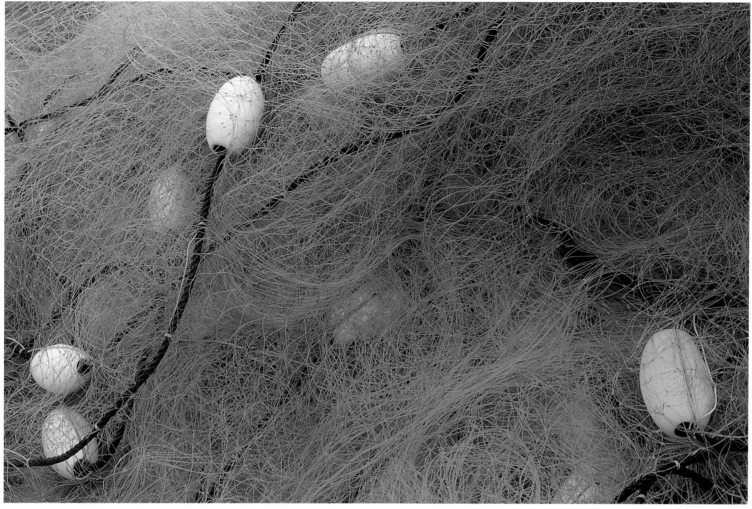

Commercial fishing nets and repair:
Barnegat Light (facing), and Manasquan
River, Point Pleasant Beach (left).

51

Barnegat Inlet (above, and facing, top). Surf fishing, Harvey Cedars (facing).

And all I ask is a windy day with the white clouds flying, And the flung spray and the blown spume, and the sea gulls crying.

— *John Masefield*

PHOTOGRAPHS BY DAVID BARBARA (above) and SUSAN HILL (below)

53

PHOTOGRAPH BY PATTI KELLY

I am fevered with the sunset,
I am fretful with the bay,
For the wander-thirst is on me...

— *Richard Hovey*

Island Beach State Park dunes (left).
Long Beach Island (facing). Ventnor
City Fishing Pier (below).

PHOTOGRAPHS BY RICK VIZZI (above) and DONALD T. KELLY (below)

PHOTOGRAPHS BY DONALD T. KELLY (above) and RAY FISK (below)

*Long Beach Island (above). Ocean City
(facing, above). Windsurfing, Barnegat Bay,
off Harvey Cedars (facing, bottom).*

For winter's rains and ruins are over.

— *William Shakespeare*

Bonnet Island, on the causeway to Long Beach Island (facing and left). Barnegat Light (above).

PHOTOGRAPH BY SALLY VENNEL

Summer

*Beach umbrella, Beach Haven. Gulls
at sunset, Barnegat Light (facing).*

There is no lover like an island shore for lingering embrace,
No tryst as faithful as the turning tide at its accustomed place.

— *Elizabeth Cutter*

Beach scene, Atlantic City.

By Sandy Gingras

Oh, summertime, you are an invitation, a seduction. I am so lusciously confused by you. I've lost my sense of time; I put it down somewhere next to that book I was reading, next to the sweating glass of iced tea. I am grown up; I'm a child. I don't know what I am. What was I thinking, what was I saying…? Summertime: You sway me on the hammock, dance with me to that old Van Morrison song, elongate my hours, dip me in and out of afternoon naps. You hum to me with bees, sugar the air with flowers, lullaby the surf. You pull the tide out, stretch the longest day. I'm a body of languor. I'm humid; I'm yawning. But don't let me sleep through it. See how I'm burning? Put some lotion on my back. Please. Because under the quiet, summertime, you are urgent and pushy and I can't hold onto you. June…July…August, you are zero to sixty and gone. You melt the asphalt. There's not enough ozone in the world to block you. Your flowers open and are done. Your colors are glare. Everything at the farm market is ripe at once. There are mountains of white corn, acres of peaches. The world is ready, ready, ready. Don't waste it.

Look how the morning waits for us pink as a promise. Come out into it. Just sit

Spray Beach, Long Beach Island.

PHOTOGRAPH BY MICHAEL BAYTOFF

PHOTOGRAPHS BY RAY FISK (above) and PATTI KELLY (below)

What are the wild waves saying,
Sister, the whole day long?

— *Joseph Edwards Carpenter*

*Boogieboarder, Harvey Cedars, and
sea stars, Long Beach Island. Beach
reflections, Ventnor (facing).*

64

on the porch with a mug of coffee and watch it becoming. The wind gathers itself from sleep, an egret stalks the salt marsh. That vine is winding itself into knots and flowers. The air holds the smell of bacon frying, draws out the laugh of that gull, echoes the cheap, innocent slap of a flip-flop. Don't be distracted. Don't go and do something else. The world is full of pause. See that fisherman balanced on the horizon in his little boat? I can hear him reeling in; I'm right there with him. The air trapezes us over, connects us. He's humming some song that everyone knows. Hear how it goes?

Wait a bit and the morning murmurs with far-off engines starting. Come churn through the wide possibility of water. Carve through the channel markers. It's a world out here of currents and washes. There are schools moving underneath us, birds tracking above, gnats making their own clouds. Every boat leaves a wake. Each sandbar raises an obstacle. Those are the pilings of history…that's where Johnny's hunting shack was, that's the skeleton of the old fish factory, there's the cove where Blackbeard hid. Under this bay are sunken things. Watch out for them — the treasures and the ruins both — they shift and rise. Only the baymen still know the stories nailed into those boards. Listen to how the marsh clicks and slurps, burbles and whispers. Summer is thick with a yearning song. Simplicity: I don't think it's easy. Drift or full ahead — all we can do is navigate by feel.

Afternoon is full of itself — turn up the color, open the breeze. The beach beckons and glitters — all sensations arrayed. Try to take it in…but it's a too big sun in a too big sky. Every beach is a postcard — wish you were here! The people

PHOTOGRAPH BY CHARLES ARLIA

I too saw the reflection of the
summer sky in the water.

— *Walt Whitman*

look so various but similar. Here they dart and dive, boogie and strut, nap and dream. They are philosophers and litterers. They are burned in odd stripes and sticky and sun-blocked. Feel the heat of it! How electric the air really is. How it smells like something cooking up. Even in the quietest moment, there's amusement park in the air. There's the wide open throttle of a flower. There's Coppertone and barbecue. There's the gushy, tangy, spiritual wash of the sea. There's a skid in the road. You can't deny it. Summer wears the bikini, makes its own parade, can't stop staring. Summer: All you need is a heart to run you all day. All you need is a body.

The day lengthens and lengthens until there are only moments left in the slant of the sun. The world leans toward shade. The beach is soft with old castles and the dimples of footprints. A lone fisherman casts into the pink waves. Sandpipers cut the low sky. Let's go home: take the best shells

PHOTOGRAPH BY REBECCA BARGER

Ocean City Boardwalk arcade and surfer (left).
Least tern feeding young, Stone Harbor (facing).
Boardwalk feeding, Ocean City (facing, above).

PHOTOGRAPHS BY REBECCA BARGER (above) and STEVE GREER (below)

and hang the wet towels on the line. The outside shower runs like rain. We are cleaner than we've ever been before. Dinner is a picnic: pass the corn, pass the salt, the pepper and the butter. We are sunburned and filled with good stories. We are interrupting each other, did you see that wave, did you see that ride? Let's use the paper plates and set up the kid's table. We are too many people, not enough beds, abundantly content. We troop like a circus to the bay to see the sun set. Just stand there and watch. It's enough. Believe me. Believe me.

When night moves in, the sky is stirred with stars. Two bikes clickity swish down a road. A sailboat line slings some song about lonesome. A dock shifts in the whir of a tide change. Someone is doing the dishes in the house down the street. Someone let the screen door bang. Someone is walking on pebbles, slapping down a hand of rummy, getting dressed to go dancing. Summer has its windows open: Listen in on conversations and crickets; smell the dense breath of the sea. The sheer curtains are rollicking like ghosts. On this summer night, there's laughter carrying, a car going past, two people watching the moon. There's a bed of relief, a road that goes on to trouble. It's all here. I tell you, it's all here.

Summer's lease hath all too short a date.

— *William Shakespeare*

*Beach scenes, Long Beach Island (above),
and Ocean City (facing).*

A life on the ocean wave,
a home in the rolling deep.

— *Epes Sargent*

Lifeguard races: Brant Beach, Long Beach Island (below), and Sandy Hook (facing); rowing in surf, Atlantic City (right).

PHOTOGRAPHS BY DONALD T. KELLY (above) and RAY FISK (below)

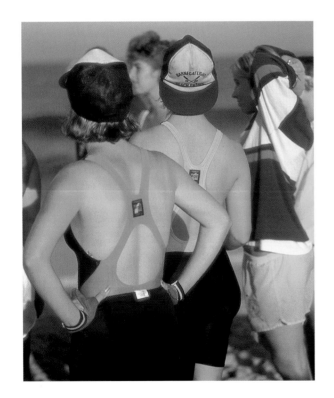

I was sired among the surges,
I was cubbed beside the foam;
All my heart is in its verges,
And the sea wind is my home.

— *Bliss Carman*

PHOTOGRAPH BY RAY FISK

PHOTOGRAPH BY NANCY L. ERICKSON

PHOTOGRAPHS BY SUSAN HILL (above) and DONALD T. KELLY (left)

Summer colors: Cape May (facing),
Hereford Inlet Light, North Wildwood
(above, left), Cape May dunes (left),
and Harvey Cedars (above).

Safe harbor and shelter: Beach Haven (right), Ocean Grove (below), Loveladies (facing, right), and along the Delaware Bay near East Point (facing, below).

And there be some who
say that sunk ships rise
To seek familiar harbors
in the night.

— *David Morton*

PHOTOGRAPHS BY RAY FISK (above) and DANIEL LEACH (below)

PHOTOGRAPH BY CORNELIUS HOGENBIRK

Crabbing boat (above), and clammer in garvey, Barnegat Bay (facing). Yellow-crowned night heron with crab, Island Beach State Park (facing). Tidal creek and salt marsh, Cape May County (facing, above).

PHOTOGRAPHS BY DANIEL LEACH (above) and RAY FISK (below)

PHOTOGRAPH BY RICH A. KING

The mussel-pooled and
heron-priested shore.

— *Dylan Thomas*

PHOTOGRAPHS BY SALLY VENNEL (above) and STEVE GREER (below)

Ocean City beach (above). Nesting gull and chick, Cape May County (facing). Juvenile gull with sea star, and American oystercatcher, Barnegat Light (facing, above).

PHOTOGRAPHS BY RAY FISK (left), DONALD T. KELLY (above) and DAVID LORENZ WINSTON (below)

PHOTOGRAPH BY WILLIAM A. BRETZGER

Wildwood beach scene (above), and lifeguards (facing). Laughing gull in flight, Cape May, and kite flyers, Harvey Cedars (facing).

E-scow sailboat race, Little Egg Harbor Bay (above).
Catamaran race, Barnegat Bay (facing).

PHOTOGRAPH BY RAY FISK

As idle as a painted ship
upon a painted ocean.

— *Samuel Taylor Coleridge*

Speed, bonny boat, like a
bird on the wing.

— *H.F. Boulton*

Catboat race, off Harvey Cedars (above). Catboat, Barnegat Bay, and boat and wake, Little Egg Harbor Bay (facing).

PHOTOGRAPH BY RAY FISK

Traditional Barnegat Bay catboats, off Long Beach Island (above), and sailboarders at sunset, Little Egg Harbor Bay (facing).

Blow me about in winds.

— William Shakespeare

The people along the sand
All turn and look one way.
They turn their back on the land.
They look at the sea all day.

— *Robert Frost*

*Long Beach Island surf (above), and
skimboarders, Monmouth Beach (facing).*

A mile of warm,
sea-scented beach.

— *Robert Browning*

PHOTOGRAPHS BY RAY FISK (below) and DONALD T. KELLY (right)

Relaxation, Margate (right). Atlantic City beach (facing). Snapper blue, Long Beach Island (below), and prize blue marlin, Beach Haven (facing).

The sea was wet
as wet could be,
The sands were dry as dry.
You could not
see a cloud, because
No cloud was in the sky.

— *Lewis Carroll*

PHOTOGRAPHS BY RAY FISK

Little Egg Harbor Bay, off Beach Haven (above), and diamondback terrapin on cedar piling (right). Ship Bottom beach (facing, above), Cape May beach with pod of dolphins near shore (facing).

For the call of the running tide
Is a wild call and a clear call
that may not be denied.

— *John Masefield*

PHOTOGRAPHS BY RAY FISK (above) and JUDIE LYNN (below)

PHOTOGRAPHS BY PATTI KELLY (above) and REBECCA BARGER (below)

I love, oh! how I love to ride
On the fierce, frowning, bursting tide.

— Barry Cornwall

Surfing: Ocean City (above, and facing, left),
and Long Beach Island (facing, above).

PHOTOGRAPHS BY WILLIAM A. BRETZGER

Shrine of towels, Ventnor (above).
Ocean City beach scenes (facing).

All in a hot and copper sky,
The bloody sun at noon.

— *Samuel Taylor Coleridge*

PHOTOGRAPH BY MICHAEL S. MILLER

Lifeguards, Avon-by-the Sea (above). Beach scenes: Beach Haven (facing) and Harvey Cedars (facing, right).

There's a magic in
the distance where the
sea-line meets the sky.

— *Alfred Noyes*

PHOTOGRAPHS BY RAY FISK

PHOTOGRAPHS BY WILLIAM A. BRETZGER (above), RAY FISK (below) and DANIEL LEACH (below right)

Ocean City beach scene (above). Avon-by-the-Sea boardwalk and beach (facing, above). Beach read, Harvey Cedars; and laughing gulls, Cape May (facing).

PHOTOGRAPH BY PETER KEENEN O'BRIEN

PHOTOGRAPHS BY THOMAS A. McGUIRE (above), CHARLES ARLIA (below) and RICH VIZZI (below right)

Atlantic City beach reflection (left); jellyfish polyp, Island Beach State Park (above); surf boat, Cape May (top). Sunset at Cape May (facing).

PHOTOGRAPH BY MICHAEL BAYTOFF

PHOTOGRAPHS BY PETER KEENEN O'BRIEN (above) and THOMAS A. McGUIRE (below)

Thunderstorm off Wildwood Crest (above), Ocean City storm (left). Summer northeaster, Spray Beach, Long Beach Island (facing).

Night sank upon the dusky beach, and on the purple sea.

— *Thomas Babington Macauley*

PHOTOGRAPHS BY WILLIAM A. BRETZGER (above) and SUSAN HILL (below)

Day's end: Barnegat Light (above), and Ship Bottom beach
(facing). Seining at sunset, Harvey Cedars (facing).

PHOTOGRAPH BY DON MERWIN

PHOTOGRAPH BY DONALD T. KELLY

Seaside Heights boardwalk (right); club scene, Beach Haven (below). Atlantic City Boardwalk, and Cape May moonrise (facing).

'Cause down the shore everything's all right, you and your baby on a Saturday night.

— *Bruce Springsteen*

109

Let's have one
other gaudy night.

— *William Shakespeare*

Fourth of July fireworks: Seaside Heights (above), and Ocean City (facing). Boardwalk scene, Wildwood (facing).

PHOTOGRAPH BY DONALD T. KELLY

PHOTOGRAPHS BY WILLIAM BRETZGER (above) and CHARLES ARLIA (below)

What hath night to
do with sleep?

— *John Milton*

PHOTOGRAPHS BY DANIEL ROGERS (above) and RICK VIZZI (below)

Dusk falls on the Shore:
Barnegat Light (above), and
Ocean City (left, and facing).

113

My life is like a stroll upon the beach, as near the ocean's edge as I can get.

— Henry David Thoreau

PHOTOGRAPH BY PETER KEENEN O'BRIEN

PHOTOGRAPHS BY FRANK VARKALA (above) and REBECCA BARGER (below)

A pleasant walk,
a pleasant talk,
along the briny beach.

— *Lewis Carroll*

Beach scenes: Surf City (above), Ocean City (left), Cape May (facing).

115

Striped bass catch,
Barnegat Light.

Autumn

By Larry Savadove

Fall comes to the shore in small sighs and apologies, as if it knows it doesn't belong. The shore is where summer lives. No one sings "Autumn at the Shore." There are precious few leaves to paint, just a quick sweep of goldenrod over the dunes. All else is earlying evenings and doles of rain. People flee, heading south, pursuing summer.

But to dwellers by the sea, fall is relief, and belief. The beach no longer smells of coconut oil. It is primeval again. Looking seaward, you recognize eternity. Houses stand empty-eyed. Gulls squawk at tire tracks in the sand until they, too, are gone. The sea darkens, but the sky lifts. You can stand on the beach and cast a line and connect with the deepest abyss. You can surf a wave of your own, named and claimed. You can kayak out with the porpoises and pelicans, just that.

The sand fills in summer footprints until only yours remain. It's cool underfoot, as if the core of the earth were pulling into hibernation. Your shadow reaches out over the waves to meet the moon. You can hear the dune grasses strum. You can hear the wing beats of migrating ducks high in the sunset and the soft calls of overnighting geese. Shore birds leave. The laughing gulls slowly pull off their black hoods to blend feathers with the sky that will carry them away. Piping plovers flee the rumors that blow down from the north pole. Egrets suddenly find memories of distant bayous in their eyes, and maps to get there. High in some unreachable stratosphere, icy arrows point the way.

But the air that chills also sparks. Stars that lay hidden in the summer earthglow emerge again, reminding us we're not alone. We walk down the middle of the street and are surprised by a stray car, reminding us how alone we are. Boats retreat into their cocoons. The bay is redolent with the pungent perfume of dank mud and old bait and rotting vegetation. Whiffs of wood smoke delight with a primal comfort. The seawind draws patterns in the shifting sands, spreading a carpet of arabesques. It tidies up the sky, too, pushing the dust and pollen and fumes of summer somewhere off the edge of the world.

PHOTOGRAPHS BY FRANK L. VARKALA (below) and DONALD T. KELLY (above)

Dockmaster's shed, Barnegat Light, Corson's Inlet State Park, Upper Township (opposite). Surf fishing, Barnegat Light (above).

Days shrink before we're done with them. In the sea the waves reflect the lowering light in shades of deep aqua and turquoise. They form moving sculptures, uninterrupted by flesh or Styrofoam, slowly enough to imprint their supple geometries on that gallery we all carry in our heads. You must look quickly, though; they will not heed your plea to "stay...stay a moment."

But you can walk for miles and be alone with your thoughts, or your god.

Still, it is not for everyone. "It's shifty." "Nothing's open." "It's...sad." It is also the time when the ancient god Hurakan walks up the coast chewing pieces out of the shoreline, leaving ruined palaces behind and fouling the air with its breath.

But living in a place without seasons is like living by a sea that is always calm. Seasons provide both certainties and surprises. And they teach us lessons: Spring is exuberant, anything is possible. Summer is satisfaction, life has its own rewards. Winter is wary, watch your step. These are the emotional seasons.

Fall is deception. It's the time of year when peaches turn mealy, when corn turns horsey, when melons smell of sweet rot. The air is not just bracing, it's biting. Hungry owls fly out in the twilight,

PHOTOGRAPH BY PATTI KELLY

Holgate, Long Beach Island, Edwin B. Forsythe National Wildlife Refuge (above). Corson's Inlet State Park.

When the wind is in the north,
The skillful fisher goes not forth;
When the wind is in the south
It blows the bait in the fish's mouth.

— *Old folk rhyme*

*Surf fishing, Long Beach Island, (above), and
Barnegat Light (right).*

the moon is more steadfast than the sun and everybody smiles bravely and says, "I just love fall." You find yourself testing the shutters, oiling the hinges, piling the porch rockers in the outdoor shower and emptying the outdoor pipes. You suddenly coddle the house plants. You look for driftwood for the fire. You air out the corduroys and the woolies to leach the linger of mothballs, make thick soups and hot rums. You step on the shushing sand, and try to recall the summer beach, urgent with children.

Fall is a season for the mind, the time when realities overtake summer fantasies: youth does not last forever; the sun does not always warm us; days shrink; nights threaten. Joys become memories and memories crinkle and dry. There is nothing that does not change: the air, the shifting reeds, the earth itself.

Fall stirs all the dreads of life. No? Try putting Halloween in May. Or getting married in October. We respond to the messages our senses deliver. We see the fade, blossoms withering, life seeping away. We listen to the rattle of hollow reeds and the cough of the wind at the window. We feel the heat of the world thin to a rumor, then dissolve. We taste the staleness in the morning air.

Fall is the time for reflection. The Jews put Yom Kippur in the fall, the Day of Atonement when you recall and regret all your sins. In Mexico, the Day of the Dead comes in the fall, when your ancestors return to see how you're doing. And, of course, there's Halloween, to

remind us that nothing stays, everything moves, only the grave is forever.

There are harvest festivals in the fall, but they only celebrate the hope of surviving winter. We revel when the leaves burst into bright crimson, but it is not a reaffirmation, only a dying flush. Our ancient ancestors were never sure that the earth would reawaken. They devised rituals and ruses to help. They attached names to the powers and then begged them for mercy. They felt forces before they knew them: the earth turning under their feet, cycles spinning over their heads, a spirit that transcended mortality until they began to discern some order, even some reassurance. But they never took it for granted.

The gut reacts to fall, to what the senses inform, and it tightens and trembles. But it is a triumphant time for the mind. Because now that we know what happens, we can relax, enjoy the change and the wait. We can anticipate, not cower. The mind ranges beyond the seasons. The mind accepts the deaths for what they are — rests, adjustments, preludes. The senses bring us no proof of this. But the mind can store messages from other times, sort through them: there will be a winter first, hard, cold and blear, but then a spring, with all the promise returned. We can contemplate futures, make plans. We can feel the touch of a hand of an ancient ancestor, reassuring: "It's all right. Nothing dies, only sleeps. We know. You'll see."

Fall is the season that makes us human.

PHOTOGRAPH BY ROB PIETRI

PHOTOGRAPHS BY RAY FISK

Commercial net fishing, offshore of Cape May (above and left). Oyster Creek docks, Atlantic County (facing).

PHOTOGRAPHS BY RAY FISK (above and below) and RICH A. KING (below left)

Highlands and the Twin Lights of the Navesink Lighthouse (above). Commercial fishing fleet, Cape May, and lobster pot boat (facing). Striped bass catch, Island Beach State Park (facing).

127

PHOTOGRAPHS BY ROB PIETRI (above) and PATTI KELLY (below)

PHOTOGRAPHS BY NANCY L. ERICKSON (above) and RAY FISK (below)

Jetty fishing, Longport (above). Commercial fishing boat, Barnegat Light (left). Mullica River crab house, Oyster Creek (facing, top). Garvey, Barnegat Bay (facing, bottom).

There is as good fish in the
sea as ever came out of it

— *Sir Walter Scott*

129

PHOTOGRAPHS BY RICK VIZZI (above) and PATTI KELLY (below)

Cape May Point (above). Abandoned garvey, West Creek (left). Fishing boat, Jenkins Sound, Cape May (facing).

There is nothing —
absolutely nothing — half so
much worth doing as simply
messing about in boats.

— *Kenneth Grahame*

PHOTOGRAPHS BY RAY FISK

Hobie cat, Ventnor beach (left).
Sailing off Barnegat Light (below),
and in Barnegat Bay (facing).

PHOTOGRAPHS BY RICK VIZZI (above) and RAY FISK (below)

The shore of the
sounding sea.

— Homer

PHOTOGRAPH BY ROBERT MANNERS

*Oyster Creek, Atlantic County (above). Sailboats
at dusk, Barnegat Bay, Seaside Park (facing).*

Was it for this the wild geese spread
The grey wing upon every tide?

— *William Butler Yeats*

Ducks fly near Surf City (above), and snow geese take flight in Brigantine, Forsythe National Wildlife Refuge (facing). Railbird hunting near Delaware Bay, Cumberland County (left).

Bay heather in bloom in a salt marsh, Manahawkin; seaside goldenrod attracts migrating monarch butterflies, Island Beach State Park (above). Marsh walk, Motts Creek (facing). Great egrets and snowy egrets, back bay, Island Beach State Park (facing).

PHOTOGRAPHS BY JOHN HENRICI (above) and RICH A. KING (below)

PHOTOGRAPH BY MICHAEL J. KILPATRICK

East Point Light, near the Maurice River on the Delaware Bay (above, and facing). Barnegat Lighthouse, and salt marsh with glasswort in October colors, Cedar Run (facing).

PHOTOGRAPHS BY DANIEL LEACH (above) and RAY FISK (below)

PHOTOGRAPH BY MICHAEL J. KILPATRICK

Barnegat Light (above). Cape May Light (right, and facing). Lens inside Cape May Light (facing).

PHOTOGRAPHS BY DONALD T. KELLY (above) and PETER KEENEN O'BRIEN (below)

Lead, kindly light, amid
the encircling gloom.

— *John Henry Newman*

Charm'd magic casements
opening on the foam
Of perilous seas, in faery
lands forlorn.

— *John Keats*

Cape May (left). South Seaside Park (below). Sandy Hook Light reflected (facing).

PHOTOGRAPHS BY DONALD T. KELLY

*Asbury Park (above). Amusement pier, Seaside
Heights; boardwalk shop, Cape May (facing).*

PHOTOGRAPHS BY DAVID LORENZ WINSTON (above) and RICK VIZZI (below)

She was a child and I was a child
In this kingdom by the sea.

— *Edgar Allen Poe*

147

PHOTOGRAPHS BY RAY FISK (above) and CHARLES ARLIA (below)

148

Ocean City Boardwalk (above, and facing);
Asbury Park (facing, top).

Whom do you lead on
Rapture's roadway far?

— *Frederic William Goudy*

*Island Beach State Park (above, left). Long Beach
Island causeway (above). Cape May Point and
ferry to Lewes, Delaware (facing).*

PHOTOGRAPH BY SUSAN FEDERICI

151

PHOTOGRAPH BY SALLY VENNEL

*Cape May (above). Bonnet
Island, causeway to Long
Beach Island (facing).*

Cape May porch (above). Ocean City surfer
(facing). Ship Bottom beach (facing).

So let us welcome
peaceful evening in.

— *William Cowper*

PHOTOGRAPHS BY REBECCA BARGER (above) and RAY FISK (below)

Whispering vows that
only the sea keeps.

— *Walter Bargen*

PHOTOGRAPHS BY BRIEN SZABO (above) and CORNELIUS HOGENBIRK (below)

*Sandy Hook sunrise (above). Shells and surf, Sandy Hook
(facing). Holgate, Long Beach Island (facing).*

PHOTOGRAPH BY RAY FISK

Hurricane surf, Surf City (above). Stormy fishing on the Atlantic City Boardwalk, and a foggy Sea Girt Boardwalk (facing).

The sea, unmated creature, tired and lone,
Makes on its desolate sands eternal moan.

— *Percy Bysshe Shelley*

158

Have you been at sea on a windy day
When the water's blue
And the sky is too,
And showers of spray
Come sweeping the decks
And the sea is dotted
With little flecks
Of foam, like daisies gay.

— *Winifred Howard*

In the sweet by-and-by, we shall meet
on that beautiful shore.

— *Hymn*

160

Barnegat Light beach path (left). Old sign, Long Beach Island causeway (above). Holgate beach, Long Beach Island (facing); commercial fishing, offshore Cape May (facing).

PHOTOGRAPHS BY RAY FISK (above), RICH KING (below left) and MICHAEL KILPATRICK (below right)

PHOTOGRAPHS BY SALLY VENNEL (above) and RAY FISK (below)

Long Beach Island causeway (above); Barnegat Bay, Harvey Cedars (right, and facing, top). Osprey ("fish hawk") with weakfish, Island Beach State Park; loggerhead turtle skull, Dennis Creek Wildlife Management Area, Cape May County (facing).

Dune grass and primary dunes: Island Beach State Park (above, and facing), Barnegat Light (left).

165

*Seaside goldenrod and poison ivy
(above). Red fox, beach and dunes,
Barnegat Light (facing).*

PHOTOGRAPHS BY EDWARD M. KULBACK and RAY FISK (below)

Come unto these yellow sands,
and then take hands.

— *William Shakespeare*

167

Where the broad ocean
leans against the land.

— *Oliver Goldsmith*

Dunes, Island Beach State Park (facing).
Long Beach Island dunes (above).

PHOTOGRAPH BY J.J. RAIA

Autumn evening, and the morn
When the golden mists are born.

— *Percy Bysshe Shelley*

Island Beach State Park dunes (facing).
Surf City beach (above).

Barnegat Lighthouse in snow.

Winter

By Margaret Thomas Buchholz

My childhood home was a drafty, isolated cottage facing Barnegat Bay on the west, always cold in winter. The northwest wind whipped the water over the bulkhead and salt spray speckled the windows. In my imagination, the accumulating clouds hovering over the mainland took the shape of Aeolus, Greek god of the winds, lips pursed, cheeks puffed up like a blowfish, exhaling an eternally long breath. His powerful gust transformed the slate water, urged the waves to dance and leap, then rush across the bay until they met the resistant bulkhead.

Salt spray made the windows opaque; it didn't form pretty patterns the way frost did. At bedtime, after my mother turned out the light, I used to spit on my bedroom window, helping Jack Frost like an apprentice elf. If I splattered a spray of spittle with my tongue between my lips, the design on the window looked like a magnified snowflake when it froze. A drool, however, was unpredictable. Once it froze so straight it looked like my father's spine, etched high and white on his back when he bent over to pull up his long, winter underwear.

We had no central heating. On the coldest nights, I fought with my brother over who would get the thick, rough Hudson Bay blanket, striped in red, green and black. The loser got Daddy's navy pea coat; I can still feel the weight of it. Sometimes, when the temperature dropped below zero, my brother slept with our parents and I got all the extra blankets. Then I was allowed to wear my underwear and socks to bed under my flannel nightgown. I would lie on my back, solemn and still as a mummy, while my mother piled on the layers: cotton sheet, flannelette blanket, wool blanket, Grandmother's patchwork quilt. And after she kissed me goodnight, my cat Greypuss crawled through a minute opening next to my neck, slithered along my body and curled around my ankles, securely tented for the night.

White and red were the colors of those frigid winters. The frozen, crystal white bay, snowy white yard, frosty white windows and vaporous white breath. Red was the stove in the morning, a bulbous iron potbelly in the middle of the room. Daddy had to get up early, shake

Island Beach State Park (above); Bonnet Island, Long Beach Island causeway (facing, above), and Harvey Cedars beach (facing).

Lastly came Winter, clothed all in frieze.

— *Edmund Spenser*

PHOTOGRAPHS BY THOMAS J. CONNOR, JR. (above) and RAY FISK (below)

PHOTOGRAPHS BY SUSAN HILL (above) and PATTI KELLY (below)

*Viking Village, at the Eighteenth Street docks, Barnegat
Light (above). Rental boats, Manahawkin (facing, top),
and at Polly's Dock, Beach Haven (facing, below).*

down the ashes, put on more coal and open the draft. In less than ten minutes the bottom half was glowing as hot and red as my mother's lipstick or the holly berries in the garden. Eventually the heat radiated into my bedroom and I slowly lowered the covers off my nose. I raised one hand and slid my sheepskin slippers from behind my pillow. My other hand pulled my wool plaid bathrobe from the bedside chair. I disappeared under the mound of bedclothes as I dressed in the sleep-warmed cave. Then, I would spring from my nest and in two leaps be rotating next to the potbelly, broiling on one side and chilling on the other.

When the bay froze solid to the mainland, which it did almost every year until recently, the house was especially cold. The frigid wind moved over the ice and chilled us much as it cooled us in the summer. The repeating cycles of freeze and thaw jammed buckled plates of ice against the bulkhead. Moving ice pushed channel markers askew if it didn't lift them out altogether. A lone garvey might crunch through the ice, breaking a channel to a gunning shack. Seagulls were scarcer than in summer, but flocks of mallards, brants, mergansers and redheads clustered along the shore, grateful for a handful of breadcrumbs.

Now I am back in this house, but with protection against winter: trees, tall fences, insulation and thermopane windows. The land between the house and the bay has been filled, and beach grass grows between the deck and bulkhead. When the spray freezes on each spike, the yard becomes a field of gracefully arched icicles, reflecting the glimmering winter sun.

Winter air is so clear a sunset transforms the sky over the bay into a pink bowl glazed with gold and orange, then quickly moves to deep purple, stripes of cerulean, and intense blue deepening to a lesser black. When a midwinter sun lowers, it radiates onto the frozen bay. Its reflection colors earth and sky, turning it into one bright, swirling mass of energy. Flames seem to burst from west-facing windows; the sky over the ocean glows in reflected, luminous light.

The winter beach is invigorating, visceral. If the wind — always the wind — is from the west, the dunes protect me. On a sunny winter day the beach seems wider, flatter, more expansive, the sand whiter. Flocks of scoters and gulls claim the water, floating just beyond the breakers. Formations of sandpipers swirl in figure-eights as they lift from a jetty then settle again. Mares-tails of foam stream off the breakers to the east. A solitary line of footprints interlocks with paw-prints. Wind has softened the edges of four-wheel drive vehicle tracks. An incoming wave reshapes a patch of shells with a rattling, clacking sound. Down the beach, in the distance, black-clad surfers cluster like the ducks.

If a northeast wind is blowing, the churning surf pushes to the foot of the dune, carving low cliffs layered with varying shades of sandy stripes. I stand bent against the gritty wind and watch the

Beach erosion, Mantoloking.

Oh give me the flashing brine,
The spray and the ocean's roar.

— *Epes Sargent*

PHOTOGRAPH BY JUDIE LYNN

The ways deep and the weather sharp, the very dead of winter.

— *T.S.Eliot*

PHOTOGRAPH BY ROB PIETRI

180

Marina, Great Bay Wildlife Management Area (above). Iced-in pilings, Sandy Hook (facing). Water vapor rises from surf, Point Pleasant Beach, (facing).

turbulent breakers, white as far as the horizon. Early in the morning, ice frosts the jetties and sea smoke hovers over the water. The beach is swept clean, then left with a new wrack line of sea-borne detritus. I find a sturdy waterlogged timber with rusty iron spikes, remnant of a shipwreck or a storm-dismembered seawall. When the winter-hardened sand freezes it crunches as I step, collapsing underfoot.

A coastal blizzard leaves the beach so white the sand becomes gray by contrast. A veil of white obliterates beachfront homes. Snow fills gullies in the rock jetties and hugs the dunes. Children would sled down them if they were allowed. I used to. Now cross-country skiers glide along the edge of the surf.

On some beaches seawalls and boardwalks have usurped the dunes. Behind the seawalls, boarded beach cabanas and empty condominiums front the ocean, shuttered against winter storms. Along the boardwalk, a congregation of white-bellied gulls faces into the wind, defining its direction. Runners buck this wind, or speed before it. In red and yellow parkas, they sparkle on the gray ribbon of boards. Two men lounge on a bench in the sunny niche of a closed concession stand and look longingly at an empty fishing pier projecting into the pewter sea. A cold sun only hints at warmth.

Amusement parks are static, giant immobile sculptures, steely and cold. Marinas display plastic wrapped boats. Motels are barren. Traffic lights on broad ocean avenues blink at very few cars. A flock of Canada geese waddles across an intersection; a formation of cyclists, bent low over handlebars, glides around them. Rows of Cape Cod cottages, angled modern homes, pastel Victorian concoctions and sprawling, multi-porch shingle palaces line quiet streets. They are empty and cold, pipes drained. Up and down the coast, tens of thousands of rooms quietly wait for summer.

And those of us here all winter — are we cold, static and quietly waiting for summer? I am so often asked, "What do you do down there all winter?" I might answer flippantly, "I save your place." But the handfuls of families who keep a few lights burning on each deserted street are very happy when the crowds leave. We do the same things you do in your winter hometowns: cook, drink, argue, make love, read, watch TV, go to movies, have dinner parties, plan next year's garden, ferry kids to activities, attend high-school basketball games, bitch about the government, work for our favorite organization. The facets of a life at the winter shore are the same as inland. But we live in a greater space. It's good for our souls to have all that water before our eyes. Especially in the winter.

Island Beach State Park.

PHOTOGRAPH BY GENE AHRENS

On the shores of darkness there is light.

— *John Keats*

*Barnegat Bay, Harvey Cedars (facing), and
foggy morning, Ocean City (left).*

185

Cross-beach skiing (above), "bay hockey", and
beach walk, Harvey Cedars (facing).

Colder and louder blew the wind,
A gale from the North-east;
The snow fell hissing in the brine,
And the billows frothed like yeast.

— *Henry Wadsworth Longfellow*

PHOTOGRAPHS BY RAY FISK

PHOTOGRAPH BY THOMAS A. McGUIRE

There is a rapture on the lonely shore...
By the deep sea, and music in its roar.

— *Lord Byron*

PHOTOGRAPHS BY NANCY L. ERICKSON (above) and JUDIE LYNN (below)

Atlantic City surfers (above);
Point Pleasant Beach (right);
Wildwood beach (facing).

PHOTOGRAPH BY THOMAS A. McGUIRE

Ocean Grove (facing); Snow-covered dunes, Cape May (above).

Some unsuspected
isle in far-off seas.

— *Robert Browning*

PHOTOGRAPH BY RAY FISK

Moonrise over dunes, Barnegat Lighthouse State Park (above); North Beach, Long Beach Island, beachfront (facing). Asbury Park Convention Hall and boardwalk (next pages).

What freezings have I felt, what dark days seen!
What old December's bareness everywhere.

— *William Shakespeare*

CONVENTION HALL

195

PHOTOGRAPH BY MIKE JONES

196

Skiing near Ocean City's Music Pier (above).
Snowy boardwalk, Seaside Heights (facing).

Silently, like tired ghosts,
The fishing fleet comes home.

— *Isabel Butchart*

PHOTOGRAPHS BY RAY FISK (above) and RICK VIZZI (below)

*Fishing boats, Barnegat Light.
Commercial boat leaves Barnegat Inlet
(facing, above). Ice-shrouded wreck,
Brigantine (facing).*

PHOTOGRAPHS BY PAT TOTTEN (above) and SUSAN HILL (below)

*Frozen rowboat, Holgate
(above); gill-net boat,
Barnegat Light (right).
Commercial fishing fleet,
Point Pleasant (facing).*

*Commercial fishing boat in a frozen Navesink River
with Twin Lights lighthouse on the Highlands beyond.*

Lost as a candle lit at noon,
Lost as a snowflake in the sea.

— *Sara Teasdale*

East Point Light, Delaware Bay (above).
Barnegat Light (facing).

PHOTOGRAPH BY ROB PIETRI

PHOTOGRAPHS BY DAN RYAN (above) and ROSEMARY A. DXON (below)

Twin Lights of the Navesink, Highlands (above and left). Sea Girt Light (facing).

PHOTOGRAPH BY DAN RYAN

PHOTOGRAPHS BY DONALD T. KELLY (above) and BOB BIRDSALL (below)

*Absecon Light, Atlantic City (above); Barnegat
Light (left); Sandy Hook Light (facing).*

209

PHOTOGRAPHS BY JUDIE LYNN (above) and RAY FISK (below)

PHOTOGRAPH BY MIKE JONES

Dunes (above), and a male northern harrier — marsh hawk — (left), Island Beach State Park. Gulls in snow, Point Pleasant Beach (facing), and ocean and dunes, Loveladies, Long Beach Island (facing, below).

PHOTOGRAPH BY RICH A. KING

Arctic sea smoke rises off the ocean, Long Beach Island. Beach walk in off-shore winds, Atlantic City (facing).

PHOTOGRAPH BY CHARLES ARLIA

Surf clams: Surf City (above), and North Wildwood (facing).
Dunes and tracks, Island Beach State Park (facing, right).

PHOTOGRAPHS BY MICHAEL J. KILPATRICK (left) and J.J. RAIA (right)

215

Contributors

Fall surfing, Long Beach Island

Gene Ahrens photographed the United States and Canada with a 4x5 Linhof Technika camera for four decades. Specializing in landscapes and nature, his stock also includes all 48 contiguous U.S. states and each state capitol.

Charles Arlia of Margate has been making fine art, abstract, and scenic photographs since the early 1980s and his work is often found on display in juried shows at the Atlantic City and Ocean City art centers.

David Barbara has traveled the Jersey Shore to photograph marine life and coastal scenics since 1991. He gives lectures on whales, dolphins, porpoises, and cetaceans to many organizations and lives in Edison.

Rebecca Barger, a staff photojournalist for *The Philadelphia Inquirer* since 1985, has been nominated for two Pulitzer Prizes. She has traveled to 45 countries, however always finds time to vacation at the New Jersey shore.

Michael Baytoff's photography has appeared in numerous national and international publications such as *Time, Natural History, Audubon,* and *Wildlife Conservation* as well as exhibitions including a traveling *National Geographic* environmental exhibit. A photojournalist specializing in documentary and environmental work, he is affiliated with the Black Star agency in New York.

Bob Birdsall, along with his wife Jean, operates Birdsall Nature Photography in Barnegat Light. They specialize in images of the New Jersey Pinelands and the Jersey Shore.

William Bretzger is a staff photographer at *The News Journal* in Wilmington Del., where he lives. A native of Eatontown, N.J., he first picked up a camera as a journalism student at Trenton State College before studying photojournalism at Ohio University. Documenting the Civil War battlefield of Gettysburg is a long-term project he is pursuing.

Margaret Thomas Buchholz is the author of *Shipwrecks: 350 Years in the Graveyard of the Atlantic* (2004), co-author of *Great Storms of the Jersey Shore* (1993), editor of the historical anthology *Shore Chronicles: Diaries and Travelers' Tales from the Jersey Shore 1764-1955* (1999), all published by Down The Shore Publishing, and *Seasons in the Sun,* a pictorial history. She is editor of *The Beachcomber,* a weekly newspaper on Long Beach Island, where she lives.

Donna Connor is a professional photographer with more than 25 years experience in photojournalism, portraiture and, most recently, travel photography. Her work has appeared in publications ranging from *People* and *Time* to *Sports Illustrated* and her clients include Atlantic City and Las Vegas casinos, numerous healthcare organizations and colleges, and an international law firm. Shooting in both corporate environments and real life situations, her love of people and the discovery of their stories makes her portraiture a collaborative effort. She resides with her family in Sweetwater, New Jersey.

Thomas Connor, a resident of Doylestown, Pa., and Beach Haven, N.J., specializes in nature studies, landscapes and seascapes. He has traveled extensively throughout North America for his subjects yet finds some of his most satisfying material along the New Jersey Shore and in the pinelands. His work is featured in various art shows and has been included in the *Down The Shore Calendar.* He was honored with first place in the Tinicum (Bucks County, Pa.) Arts Festival's 52nd annual juried exhibition for "Winter On The Island" and "Happy Days."

John T. Cunningham, described by the New Jersey Historical Commission as New Jersey's "best known popular historian" and by Rutgers University as "Mr. Jersey" when it gave him an honorary degree, has written 48 books, more than 2,000 articles and 18 documentary films on the state. His first book, *This Is New Jersey,* published in 1953, is still in print in its sixth revised edition. He is currently finishing a book on the Revolutionary War "dark winter" of 1779-80 in Morristown and is also at work on a revision of his well-known, but long out-of-print classic, *The New Jersey Shore.*

Rosemary A. Dixon, of Lanoka Harbor, N.J., is a retired C.P.A. who travels the world — from Holland to the Fiji Islands — to scuba dive and photograph (lighthouses, in particular). Her published articles and photographs about lighthouses include a recent profile of the creator of the U.S. Lighthouse postage stamp series.

Keith Drexler, of Manville, N.J., makes his living as a printing press operator, but spends his free time photographing beaches, boardwalks, and lighthouses along the Jersey Shore.

Nancy L. Erickson's photographs have appeared in numerous regional and national magazines, calendars and books. She and her husband Bill have operated New Wave Photography in Laurel Springs, N.J., since 1991.

Susan Federici, a pilot for 33 years, has been a flight instructor for most of that time, and worked as a corporate pilot for two decades. Specializing in aerial photographs, she "wanted others to see the view from a higher perspective," she says. "I have flown the Jersey Shore area for most of my life and, whether speeding over it at 35,000 feet in a jet or flying low and slow along the beach in a single engine airplane, I never tire of its beauty."

Valerie Fenelon has been taking photographs of the shore, as well as fine art portraits, for nearly 25 years and special occasions. A graduate of Moore College of Art, in Philadelphia, she operates North End Trilogy, an art gallery featuring local and shore artists, in Barnegat Light.

Ray Fisk joined college friends in 1977 to establish *The SandPaper* on Long Beach Island — his first encounter with the Jersey Shore. He worked there as Associate Editor, and then as a photojournalist for *The New York Times*, United Press International, and *The Philadelphia Inquirer* throughout the 1980s, covering Atlantic City, the shore, and southern New Jersey. He founded Down The Shore Publishing in 1984.

Sandy Gingras is the author and illustrator of *The Uh-oh Heart* (2003), *How to Live on an Island* (1996), *How to Live at the Beach* (2001), *How to be a Friend* (2003) and *Reasons to be Happy at the Beach* (2003), and is the creator of *At the Beach House: A Guest Book* (2003), all published by Down The Shore Publishing. A graduate of Hamilton College, she received an M.A. in English from Duke University and an M.A. in counseling from Rider College. The owner of "How to Live," a design and gift company and retail store in Beach Haven, she lives with her son Morgan, 14, on Long Beach Island.

Steve Greer, who grew up in the Canadian Rockies — "a magical place in which to learn the fundamentals of landscape photography," is an award winning photographer and natural history writer whose work has been featured in hundreds of publications worldwide. His images have appeared on magazine covers, calendars, greeting cards, advertising and educational materials. With an appreciation and enthusiasm for the natural world, he believes that honest, compelling photography can change the way people react to their environment, enabling them to make better decisions concerning the protection of open spaces.

Henry R. Hegeman, a resident of southern Ocean County, N.J., works for a consulting engineering firm, but has been a freelance writer and photographer for 30 years, specializing in hunting and fishing subjects. His work has appeared in numerous books, magazines, and calendars.

John Henrici is an amateur photographer residing in California, but whose heart is somewhere between Tuckerton and Leeds Point. He spent summers as a child in Lavalette, where he learned to surf, and graduated in 1976 from Stockton State College, living in and around pre-casino Atlantic City. "Invariably sunset would find me somewhere around the Mullica or Wading Rivers," he says, and he'd "follow the creeks up into the pines a bit. Rusty places. Old boats. There was simply too much to shoot. I learned to appreciate the awesome beauty of the bayshore." With his wife, Michelle, he moved to California, where they are both teachers, but "had these vivid South Jersey dreams, the residue of having stared at it so much."

Susan P. Hill-Doyle grew up on Long Beach Island and began capturing her native shore in pictures at age nine. She received a B.A. in studio art from the University of California, Santa Barbara, and now divides her time between photography, teaching elementary school art, and raising her sons Harry and Jack. Her work has appeared in numerous publications, galleries, and art shows. "Capturing a moment when everything is in perfect balance — light, subject, and atmosphere — is what my work is all about," she says.

Cornelius Hogenbirk served as a U. S. Army Signal Corps photographer in Japan during the occupation, covering the Yokohama war crimes trials. His first camera was a Brownie Hawkeye box camera, at age 10 in 1927. His scenic photographs of southern New Jersey, the Pine Barrens, and the shore have appeared in many regional publications. Retired, living in Waretown, N.J., he now devotes his time to gardening and nature photography.

Stephen Jasiecki has been photographing in the southern New Jersey shore for the past 20 years. He works as an electrician and resides in Egg Harbor Township, N.J..

Mike Jones spent ten years as a photojournalist, six of those years as the staff photographer with *The Coast Star* in Manasquan, before pursuing a full time freelance career. His father taught him to use his old Pentax SLR at age 10, and by the end of high school he was using a 4x5 Graflex. During summer vacations in Maine, he would climb around the rocky shore with a camera and tripod rather than visiting downtown Bar Harbor with his family. Currently shooting travel images and landscapes across the U.S., he makes use of a Toyo view camera and Mamiya RZ-67 medium format camera. He lives in Toms River.

With stock of over 25,000 images, **Donald T. Kelly's** nature and travel photographs have been published in formats ranging from calendars, postcards, notecards, and bookmarks to electronic media, encyclopedias, and other books and magazines, as well as displayed in exhibitions. A resident of Mays Landing, he makes his living as a union electrician, but has been a dedicated photographer for more than 25 years, selling his work professionally for the last seven. Photography is only one of his artistic passions, however; he is also a writer and painter, and has been a pianist and composer for over 30 years, having written over 100 compositions for piano, duets for piano and violin, and choral anthems.

For over a decade, photographer **Patti Kelly** has documented the environment along the Jersey Shore from the beaches to the back bays. Her award-wining work appears in magazines, newspapers, and books illustrating the people and places of New Jersey. Patti Kelly received a BA in Journalism from Temple University.

Michael J. Kilpatrick operates a nature photography guide service specializing in New Jersey coastal marsh and seashore subjects. A resident of Lindenwold, N.J., and originally from North Wildwood, his work has appeared in national publications, including *Nature Conservancy* magazine and *Ducks Unlimited*.

Rich A. King spends much of his life, since the mid-1980s, in the back bay marshes of Island Beach State Park, often sitting in a blind poised with his cameras. He is, admittedly, obsessed with the estuary, and when not making photographs there, he is giving lectures, slide shows, and educational programs on the estuary food chain, wildlife, and the bayshore environment. He makes his living as a plumber in Toms River. Of his passion for this ecosystem, he says: "What I look for is to open people's eyes."

A doctor of optometry in Freehold, **Edward Kulback**, finds his creative outlet working with his camera equipment in manual mode to "slow down the process, and think about what is being captured on film."

The nature and scenic photography of **Daniel Leach**, of Hatfield, Pa., has gone from a serious hobby in the 1980's to a part-time profession since 1996.

Manny Lekkas received his photography education at the New York Institute of Photography, has won awards for his work at numerous New Jersey art shows, and has been published in *Nature Photographer, Peterson's Photographic, New Jersey Outdoors,* and other publications. He currently resides in Winston Salem, N.C.

Burton E. Lipman's photographs have been widely published in magazines and newspapers and have won top prizes in juried contests. A resident of East Brunswick, N.J., he has had a varied career: as president and C.E.O. of a Lehman Brothers Co. subsidiary; founder and president of a heart-pacer component manufacturer; and vice-president of operations for Wyeth and Lever Brothers companies. He is also the author of technical books published by John Wiley, Prentice-Hall, and Bell Publishing.

Judie Lynn, a retail store manager in Ocean County, laments that she has little time for her photography anymore. However, with a career change into real estate, she looks forward to more flexible scheduling that will allow her to once again to pursue her passion of photography.

Robert Manners grew up in Trenton, and served as a photographer in the U.S. Army. He resided in Manahawkin for many years and now lives in Atlantic City, where he works for the Hilton Casino.

Bob Manning is employed as a Senior Business Analyst at Computer Aid Inc. in Wilmington, Del., and is a part time wedding photographer. His love of photography began in the first grade when he took a picture with an old Brownie box camera. He was influenced by his mother, who as a single parent working out of the home, supported Bob and his brother by hand coloring and painting photographs for the top photographers of the day. A graduate of the New York Institute of Photography, his photographs have been exhibited in shows from northern New Jersey to the Jersey Shore to the Pocono Mountains of Pennsylvania.

Thomas A. McGuire became an award-winning photographer, focusing on the Jersey Shore and participating in art shows throughout the state. During the 1990s, many of his images were included in the *Down The Shore* calendars. He delighted in sharing his work, and when praised for it, would say, "God created the image. I just snap it." He died in 2003, after a valiant battle with cancer, but his work lives on to inspire us.

Don Merwin resides in Cape May.

Michael S. Miller's work has been published in calendars and in local and national publications and is included in private collections and galleries. A graduate of the Art Institute of Fort Lauderdale, Fla., he is also a long-time guide for the Monmouth County Park System, and resides with his wife in Avon-by-the-Sea.

Robert S. Misewich bought his first 35mm camera while serving overseas in the army in 1960. He became a dedicated nature photographer in 1996, after retiring from a 31-year career as a field engineer with Lucent Technologies. A resident of Turnersville, N.J., his travels up and down the east coast have produced images published in *Birder's World* and other publications.

Melissa Molyneux is a freelance photojournalist in the New York region, working for magazine and newspaper clients such as the *Star Ledger, The New York Times,* and stock agencies from her home in Basking Ridge. A graduate of the Pratt Institute with a B.F.A. in photography, she studied at Central Saint Martins School of Art and Design in London. Staying true to her fine art roots she applies her fine art training to her passion for photojournalism.

Peter Keenen O'Brien has contributed to the *Down The Shore* calendars for a decade and one of his photographs appears on the cover of the novel *Tales From An Endless Summer* (1996). He follows in the footsteps of his father and grandfather as a photographer, first borrowing his father's camera for a cross-country trip during high school. Born and raised in Bayonne, he graduated from Seton Hall in 1978 and earned a masters of divinity at the university's graduate school of theology. With an interest in ecclesiastical art, he has contributed to documentaries, most recently as an associate producer on the film "An Unreliable Witness" during filming in Ireland.

Atlantic City Boardwalk

PHOTOGRAPH BY MICHAEL BAYTOFF

219

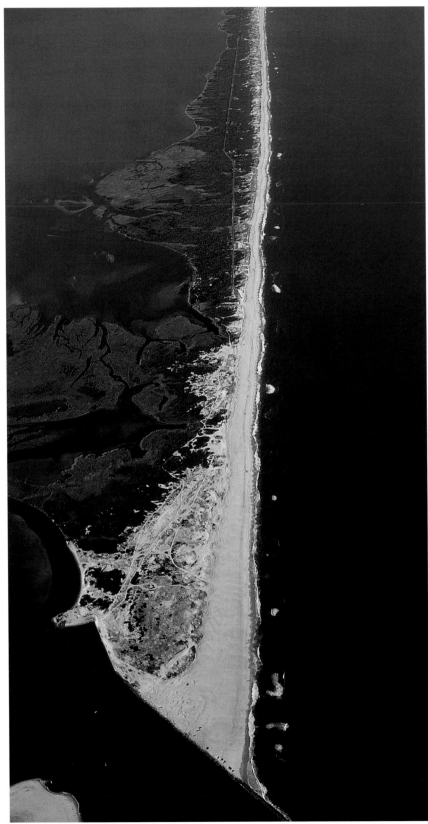

For **Rob Pietri**, the Jersey Shore was a great place to grow up in the mid 1960s and the 1970s. Summers were spent fishing with his father for stripers, blues, and blowfish or snorkeling off the jetties, spear fishing, crabbing; then, as a teen, surfing and lifeguarding. "Now, at midlife crisis stage, I am glad I can capture in my photography some of the feelings and flavors of what was once enjoyed by myself and others. Open your eyes and hear the music," he says.

Over the last ten years **J.J. Raia** has tried to photograph every corner of New Jersey in all seasons for his calendars and continues to discover new places all the time. In addition, he has now begun to photograph the landscapes of the western U.S. but continues to make a living running trains for Amtrak and lives in Edison with his wife and two children.

Dan Rogers lives in Lancaster County, Pa., and works as a construction manager but has been shooting scenic photography for almost 30 years. His serious interest in photography began while doing documentary photography as an archeologist in West Virginia.

Dan Ryan, of Highlands, N.J., has been taking pictures since his father gave him a Kodak pocket camera with flash cubes as a teenager. He works in the field of training support and incorporates photography into his work.

Larry Savadove is the author two novels — *The Oyster Singer* (2004, Down The Shore Publishing) and *The Sound of One Hand* (1960, Duell, Sloan & Pierce) — a cookbook, *Melting Pot West*, and co-author of *Great Storms of the Jersey Shore* (1993, Down The Shore Publishing). A graduate of Harvard College, he has lived in Japan, Latin America, and Los Angeles, but spent every summer of his boyhood on Long Beach Island and returned to settle there after years of wandering the world as a sailor, a soldier, a journalist, an adman, and a maker of award-winning documentaries, most notably "The Undersea World of Jacques Cousteau." His two children are also veterans of Long Beach Island; he is at work on two more novels, also set at the shore.

After working in television for over twelve years, **Brien Szabo** switched careers to become a professional nature photographer and stay-at-home dad. He specializes in capturing diverse natural images of his home state of New Jersey and the northeast. He's been published in magazines, teaches photography, and hosts nature photography workshops throughout the region.

Pat Totten has been photographing the Jersey Shore for the past 30 years. Since retiring from teaching chemistry she has traveled extensively, taking her camera to every continent to pursue her passion for photography. Much of her travel is centered around astronomical events, such as eclipses and meteor showers. In November 2003 she was part of a small group of the first humans ever to see a total solar eclipse from Antarctica.

Frank L. Varkala has concentrated on the Jersey Shore and the mountains of Vermont and New Hampshire as a photographer for 13 years, and, recently, has begun shooting casual portraits and weddings. A 1974 graduate of Fairleigh Dickinson University, and long-time resident of southern Ocean County, N.J., he now lives in Vermont.

Island Beach State Park.

Cape May sunset.

Sally Vennel and her husband divide their time between Surf City, N.J. and Crested Butte, Colo. Her work has been featured in calendars and art shows in both locations and in California. She says her photography takes her "to many beautiful places, including numerous safaris in Africa."

Rick Vizzi has been photographing nature and subjects of his interest since he was 10 and, although he received a B.A. in art from William Paterson University and Rutgers, never had "professional" jobs as a photographer other than a few years shooting weddings and some newspaper features. "I decided not to try to make a living at it, which allowed me to pursue it my way." A historic restoration contractor for almost twenty years, his latest pursuit is woodturning. His goal is to make fine prints of as many of his photographs as possible, and to exhibit them. "I have some things I'd like to communicate," he says, "more than just showing a collection of photos."

David Lorenz Winston's lifelong love of the natural landscape has taken him on travels from his home in Philadelphia throughout the U.S. and to Siberia, Peru, India, Nepal, Tibet, Greece, Portugal and Nova Scotia. His work has appeared in calendars and on cards published by Pomegranate, Brown Trout, UNICEF, the National Wildlife Federation, Hallmark, and Recycled Paper Products. He is working on the photography for a series of children's books about farm life, the first of which was the award-winning *Life on a Pig Farm* (1998, Carolrhoda Books).

Rich Youmans is a magazine and book editor who has specialized in the history and literature of the Jersey Shore. He is the editor of *Shore Stories: An Anthology of the Jersey Shore* (1998, Down The Shore Publishing); co-editor, with Frank Finale, of *Under a Gull's Wing: Poems and Photographs of the Jersey Shore* (1996, Down The Shore Publishing); and co-author, with Russell Roberts, of *Down the Jersey Shore* (1993, Rutgers University Press).

Location Index

PHOTOGRAPH BY DON MERWIN

Cape May Light.

Down The Shore Publishing offers other book and
calendar titles (with a special emphasis on the mid-Atlantic coast).
For a free catalog, or to be added to our mailing list, just send us a request:

Down The Shore Publishing
Box 3100
Harvey Cedars, NJ 08008

www.down-the-shore.com

PHOTOGRAPH BY DONALD T. KELLY

Barnegat Lighthouse and full moon.